# STUDYING
## WITH
## A
# PURPOSE

### RUDY HALL

**Remnant**
Publications

Coldwater, Michigan 49036
www.remnantpublications.com

Published by
Remnant Publications
649 East Chicago Road
Coldwater MI 49036
800-423-1319
www.remnantpublications.com

This study primarily uses the NKJV Bible.
The author encourages study with this version because
all answers are taken from this translation.

Cover designed by David Berthiaume
Copy edited by Debi Tesser
Text designed by Greg Solie • AltamontGraphics.com

ISBN: 978-1-933291-66-6

# CONTENTS

# INTRODUCTION

This book of seven Bible lessons is for everyone because it is not about joining a particular movement or church. This book isn't about convincing anyone to think like me or anyone else. It isn't about who's right or wrong in his or her personal viewpoint on Scripture. This book is about Bible-based principles on how to study to get the most out of your time spent.

I know people who have read their Bible for years and still have very little knowledge of the Scriptures. What's worse is that the Bible has had little or no effect on their lives. It is possible to go to church all of one's life and yet not have a relationship with Christ. For example, a man ran to Christ and explained that he had studied the Scriptures from his youth (all his life), and still his life lacked a relationship with God. Sad story isn't it? But it doesn't have to be that way. Christ told this man what was keeping him from having this relationship, but to him the price was too high.

This book is about studying in a way so that you can build a great relationship with Christ through the study of His Word. It's about preparing and receiving—preparing yourself to study God's promises and then expecting through faith to receive them. This book is about learning how to use the Bible as a guide to lead you through life.

There are many ups and downs in life, and God knew we could use a constant source of strength and guidance right at our finger-tips. So He gave us His Word to be that strength and guide. As you study the principles in this book, you may learn more about His will and plan for your life than you ever imagined. You will learn the key to having a progressive relationship with Christ—one that keeps on growing and growing.

After reading this book, I can't guarantee that all your questions will be answered, but I do believe you will know where the answers are and how to look for them in a way that will be revealed to you just as He inspired His chosen people to write His Word. I believe you will know how to move forward with faith and confidence rather than charge forward with no real direction. I hope this book leads you to THE BOOK—the Bible—God's Holy Word. As you read and study, my prayer is that you would truly *study with a purpose*, and may God bless you as you begin your journey with Him.

—Rudy Hall

# LESSON 1:

# Why Study?

S everal years ago a young man learned to be a builder from his father. He spent years learning the trade, both by listening to instruction and by hands-on experience. He would be praised when the job was done right, and he was corrected when the work was wrong. Since he started building at such an early age, by the time he became an adult, he was building his own houses without much difficulty.

One day he and his family moved to another state, and he decided to go into the building business on his own at the new location. He soon realized that the skill and knowledge he had was fine, but he didn't have a builder's license. In the state where he had moved, he had to acquire a license before he could build. So he bought the required books and found an ex builder who had hung up his hammer and made a living teaching seminars to people who were going after a building license.

At the time more than 50 percent of the people trying to get their licenses failed the state test. He asked the teacher, "Why are so many people failing? Is the test really that hard?" The teacher replied that it really wasn't that hard. Then the teacher also said that the people with the most experience in actually building (like he was) did the worst on the test.

Statistically, he was doomed to fail. Again, he asked the teacher why. The teacher said that it was because they forgot why they were there. He continued, "You see, all of your preconceived ideas, all of the advice you have from your father, even all the hands-on experience won't help you here." The teacher went on to say, "If you could get a license by building something, you could easily pass. But your license isn't about building; right now, it's about passing the test. If you want a license, forget what you have already learned, forget about what your father or anyone else has taught you, and pay attention to your current goal, which is to pass the state test and receive a license."

So why study? What is your goal? Here are some of the top reasons people give for studying:

1. It's good for the soul and conscience.

2. I feel better after I read the Bible.

3. It just feels right to me.

4. My pastor has told me I should study every day.

5. I would like to have more knowledge about the Bible.

6. I have a goal to read the entire Bible in one year.

These are all good reasons to a point, but let's look at just a few reasons that God gives us in His Word. You will find that God's reasons are different than man's. You have seen the top six reasons from man. Let's look at some reasons from the Bible.

1. How were the prophets inspired to write the Scriptures? 2 Peter 1:21

*"For prophecy never came by the will of man, but holy men of God spoke as they were moved by the _____ _____ ."*

✓ **NOTE: The Bible can be trusted because it is inspired by the Holy Spirit, not man. So to read a book inspired by God is one good reason to study the Bible.**

2. What type of wisdom are we promised to have if we know the Scriptures? 2 Timothy 3:15

*"That from childhood you have known the Holy Scriptures, which are able to make you wise for* __SALVATION__ *through faith which is in Christ Jesus."*

✓ **NOTE: Salvation is another very good reason to study the Scriptures.**

3. Specifically, why were these things written to us? 1 John 5:13

*"These things I have written to you who believe in the name of the Son of God, that you may know that you have* __ETERNAL LIFE__ *, and that you may continue to believe in the name of the Son of God."*

✓ **NOTE: What better goal or reason than eternal life could one have for studying? This is God's desire for us.**

4. By studying, what do we get from God? 2 Timothy 2:15

*"Be diligent to present yourself* __APPROVED__ __TO__ __GOD__ *, a worker who does not need to be ashamed, rightly dividing the word of truth."*

✓ **NOTE: Another good reason to study is to receive God's approval as God approves of those who study. The King James Version says, "Study to show thyself approved." If you look up the word "study," one definition is "intensive intellectual effort." God wants serious people reading His Word.**

5.  For what four things does God tell us the Scriptures are good? 2 Timothy 3:16

*"All Scriptures is given by inspiration of God and is profitable for _____ , for _____ , for _____ , for_____ in _____ ."*

✓ **NOTE: God doesn't want us just to read His Word. God wants us to be changed through the study of His Word. God did His part and will always continue to do so.**

We also have a part. For example:

- Doctrine or teaching: only works if you listen.

- Reproof: only works if you care.

- Correction: only works if you change.

- Righteousness: only works if you want to do right.

6.  What does the Bible say God's Word will be like to us? Psalms 119:105

*"Your word is a _____ to my feet and a _____ to my path."*

✔️ NOTE: God's Word promises to lead us on a lighted path, a path with meaning, a path approved, and a path designed by God.

7. What will the Word of God effectively do in those who believe? 1 Thessalonians 2:13

*"For this reason we also thank God without ceasing, because when you received the word of God which you heard from us, you welcomed it not as the word of men, but as it is in truth, the word of God, which also effectively* _____ *in you who believe."*

✔️ NOTE: This verse tells us the Word of God will work in us, which means we can rely on God's Word to help us in all our situations. God's Word is a source of strength for those who put it in their hearts (Psalm 40:8).

8. What kind of life does God say He wants us to have? John 10:10

*"The thief does not come except to steal, and to kill, and to destroy. I have come that they may have life, and that they may have it* _____ _____ *."*

✔️ NOTE: God alone wants you to have an abundant life. The devil wants to rob you of happiness and an enjoyable life. Gaining that abundant life is another great reason to study.

9. What does God desire for our children? Matthew 19:14

*"But Jesus said, 'Let the little children* _____
_____ _____ *and do not forbid*
*them; for of such is the* _____ _____
_____ .'"*

✓ **NOTE: Jesus wants the little children with Him, and He wants to spend time in heaven with them. One of the best reasons to study and have a relationship with Christ is not only for us, but also for our children.**

———————————— 📖 ————————————

These are just a few reasons the Bible gives us to study the Holy Scriptures, which are quite different than man's reasons. To recap, God's reasons are to give salvation, eternal life, approval, teaching, reproval, correction, instruction in righteousness, a direction in life, and a source of strength.

**To sum up, here are some great reasons to study God's Word.**

1. The Bible is God's inspired book.

2. To the sincere reader God promises salvation through His Word.

3. God's Word holds the key to eternal life.

4. We can study to show ourselves approved before God.

5. Studying will correct and change our lives from unrighteousness to righteousness.

6. God's Word is a light to guide us step by step.

7. God's Word is strength in times of need.

8. Living in accordance to God's Word means living life more abundantly.

9. Through the instruction we get in God's Word, we can teach to our children so they can have a true relationship with Christ that will last through all eternity. Our children alone should provide a heartfelt motive.

**Points not to miss before you study the Bible:**

1. Know why you're studying.

2. Know your purpose.

3. Know that God is in the business of changing hearts and lives.

4. Be ready to change.

5. The Bible, through the Spirit of God, can lead you to eternal life.

6. Take it seriously.

7. Make a commitment

So if you're ready to let God, through His Word, change your life, let's begin.

# NOTES

# LESSON 2:

# How Do I Begin?

The story is told of a small boy and his father who, after they had plowed their field in the spring, went out to pick up stones before planting. One by one they would pick up the stones and put them in large piles on the sides of the field. This was great fun for the boy. Since he was always looking for a challenge, he would always run to the largest rocks. It gave him a big sense of accomplishment to remove a large rock. In the distance he saw the largest rock yet; with great enthusiasm, he ran to pick it up but found it too big.

His father watched as his son tried harder and harder to pick it up. The little boy finally conceded that it was too big. The father said, "Son, if you use all your power, I know you can pick it up."

With renewed interest, he tried as hard as he could but just could not quite pick it up. Exhausted and discouraged, the boy sat down and said, "Father, I used all my power like you said, but I still failed.

The father replied, "No son, you haven't used all your power. You haven't asked for my help. It's within your power to ask me. If you would have just asked for my help, we could have easily moved that rock together.

1. How do we understand the things God wants us to understand? How are they revealed to us? 1 Corinthians 2:10

*"But God has revealed them to us through* _____
_____ *. For the Spirit searches all things, yes, the*
*deep things of God."*

✓ **NOTE: Also, 1 Corinthians 2:14 explains that spiritual things are spiritually discerned. So without the Holy Spirit, we cannot understand God's Word.**

2.   So how do we get the spiritual understanding? Philippians 4:6

*"Be anxious for nothing, but in everything by* _____
*and supplication, with thanksgiving, let your* _____
*be made known to God."*

✓ **NOTE: From Genesis to Revelation we are shown that great men of God were also great men of prayer. Christ Himself would spend a great amount of time in prayer with His Father. Many times we fail just like the boy in the story because we are trying to do things on our own. God tells us that the process of doing things on our own is impossible, but with God all things are possible (Matthew 19:26). The most important activity in Bible study is to *always* start your study with prayer, and ask God to reveal His Word to you through the Holy Spirit.**

3.   The Pharisees were experts in the Scriptures but only in word. They lost their focus on Christ and focused on themselves. Thus, they were no longer fit to teach or to lead even though they had a great deal of knowledge in the Scriptures. What were the people who received their spiritual instruction from the Pharisees called? Matthew 15:14

"Let them alone. They are __Blind__ leaders of the __Blind__ . And if the blind leads the blind, both will fall into a ditch."

✓ **NOTE: Without the Holy Spirit guiding us so that we just depend on ourselves and others, the Bible says our condition is blind.**

4. How do we acquire complete understanding of Bible principles? Isaiah 28:10

"For __He says__ must be upon __order on__, __Order__ upon __order__ , line __on__ __line__ , line __upon__ line, here a little, there a little."

✓ **NOTE: Don't become a one-text wonder. Don't take a Scripture verse and build your spiritual understanding upon that one verse. Many of the treasures in the Bible lie far beneath the surface and can be obtained only by diligent research and continuous effort. When studying a topic, gather all the information the Bible has on that topic: "line upon line, precept upon precept." Once you do that, you will see the complete principle and have a clearer understanding of what the Bible is saying.**

Some people pick and choose what they want to read. Some say that we should read just the New Testament, claiming that the Old Testament is outdated and done away with—not true. The Bible says all Scripture is inspired by God and given to us so we can be spiritually complete and become wise unto salvation (2 Timothy 3:15–17). When that counsel was written, the only Scriptures available were found in the Old Testament because the New Testament hadn't been written yet. Besides, much of the New Testament references the Old Testament. ALL SCRIPTURE is ALL SCRIPTURE.

5. Why were the Scriptures written in the first place? 1 Corinthians 10:11

*"Now all these things happened to them as ___example___, and they were written for our ___instruction___, upon whom the ends of the ages have come."*

✓ NOTE: Admonitions are wise words of warnings. When reading the Bible, remember for whom it was written. It was written for you; it was written for me. It was meant to be taken personally; it wasn't written just to show you other people's successes and failures. It was written for you and me today to change our lives, to teach us about Christ and His undying love for us, and to show us that He has a plan for our lives.

6. When we come to the point in our lives when we decide that we want a closer walk with God, the thought of reading and understanding the Bible may seem like a huge task. But like the father of the child picking up rocks, Christ doesn't expect or even want us to do it alone because we can't do it without His help. Also, what are we called when we start our Christian walk? 1 Peter 2:2

*"As _____  _____ , desire the pure milk of the word, that you may grow thereby."*

✓ **NOTE: Through God's Word, we can understand exactly where we are spiritually and accept our newborn condition. In Hebrews 5:13, 14, God says that He expects us to get off the milk and feed on solid food. Simply put, God expects spiritual growth. We should desire to grow in Christ, feed off the Word, and always want something more.**

So how do I begin? Begin with a desire first—a desire to have a closer walk with Christ. Next, pray for Christ to be with you, leading and guiding you into all truth. Then open His Word and receive the blessings He has in store for you—one prayer at a time and one page at a time.

**Points not to miss as you begin:**

1. Know you can't do it alone; so start by asking your heavenly Father for help (prayer).

2. Spiritual things (God and His Word) are spiritually discerned.

3. Don't be a one-text wonder. Compare Scripture with Scripture to put all the pieces together.

4. Look at the whole picture.

May God bless you as you begin your walk with Christ.

# LESSON 3:

# What Happened?

Have you ever had a relationship with a friend, spouse, or a family member, and things were great; then all of a sudden it seemed that those things had really changed? The relationship just wasn't there anymore. Many times you didn't even know why. You asked yourself, "What happened? We used to talk, share, and laugh, but that spark just isn't there anymore. Maybe it was something I said or did, or maybe it was something someone said about me."

The one thing that you knew was that something was terribly wrong, and you long for it to be right again. If someone would just tell you what the problem was, you would try to fix it. Most of us have been in that situation of knowing that something was wrong, but we do not know exactly what the problem might have been. We desperately wanted to know what happened.

The Bible tells the story of a man who was in this situation, but it was not with an earthly friend; it was with God. This man sensed that he was missing something—something was keeping him from the saving relationship that he desired. He didn't know what it was, but he knew there was a problem and desperately wanted some answers.

We do know a few things about this man. We know he was young. We know he was taught the Scriptures as a very young boy. We also know he was a very wealthy ruler. Matthew, Mark, and Luke all tell this story, but each shared details from his own point of view. Remember:

"line upon line, precept upon precept." That is how the Scriptures are to be studied.

1. Luke 18:18 tells us that this young man was a ruler. But let's look at Mark 10:17 to find out how this rich young ruler approached Christ and for what reason. What did this rich man want?

*"Now as He [Christ] was going out on the road, one came _____, _____ before Him, and asked Him, "Good Teacher, _____ _____ _____ _____ that I may inherit _____ _____ ?"*

2. What was Christ's answer? Matthew 19:17

*"So He said to him, "Why do you call Me good? No one is good but One, that is, God. But if you want to 'enter into life, _____ _____ _____."*

3. What was the response of this rich young ruler? Matthew 19:20

*"The young man said to Him, '_____ _____ things I have _____ from my youth. What do I _____ _____ ?'"*

4. What was Jesus' answer? Matthew 19:21

*"If you want to be perfect, go, _____ _____ _____ _____ and*

*give to the poor, and you will have treasure in heaven; and come, follow Me."*

5. What was the ruler's response? Matthew 19:22

*"But when the young man heard that saying, _____*

*_____  _____  _____ , for*

*he had great possessions."*

✓ **NOTE: This is an unhappy story of a man who had everything—youth, position, and wealth—yet, he knew that there was something that was keeping him from having that saving relationship with God. He went away sorrowfully, knowing what the problem was. Sadly, he figured the price was just too high.**

**Enough about him for a moment—what about you and me? What about our relationships with God? What must I do? What must you do? A close relationship with God should be our request. But first, what happened? To look at that, we need to return to the beginning, so let's go to the book of Genesis. Most of us have heard the story, but let's read the first chapter in the Bible (Genesis1:1–31). God created everything in six days—the fish, the animals, man and woman, and night and day.**

6. At the end of the six days, what did God say? Genesis 1:31

*"Then God saw everything that He had made, and indeed it was _____  _____ . So evening and morning were the sixth day."*

✓ NOTE: Everything in the Garden of Eden was perfect. Read Genesis chapter 2. God, Adam, and Eve had everything. Adam and Eve had a great marriage and a complete relationship with God. God walked with them and talked with them. He even presented the animals for Adam to see, and so he could name them (Genesis 2:19). How cool would that be? What an awesome relationship they had with God. As we continue reading, we find the relationship changed terribly.

7.   What did Adam and Eve do when they heard the Lord coming? Genesis 3:8

*"They heard the sound of the LORD God walking in the garden in the cool of the day, and Adam and His wife* _____
_____ *from the presence of the LORD God among the trees of the garden."*

✓ NOTE: Wow! What happened? The Bible is clear about what happened. Adam and Eve sinned; they disobeyed God (Genesis 3:6). That changed everything. However, God didn't forsake Adam and Eve, and He hasn't forsaken you or me. Instead, He put the plan of salvation in place, and through God's perfect plan of redemption, that perfect relationship will be restored. First, we need to define and understand what's wrong—just as the rich young ruler did. Second, we must do something about it—just as the rich young ruler *didn't*. Most of us know sin isn't good. It's a problem, but what is it exactly?

8. What is the Bible's definition of sin? 1 John 3:4

*"Whoever commits sin also sin commits lawlessness, and*

_____  _____  _____ *."*

✓ **NOTE: The King James Version simply states, "Sin is the transgression [or breaking] of the law." Now we know what sin is: it is the breaking of God's law.**

9. What exactly does breaking God's law do? Isaiah 59:2

*"But your iniquities [sin] have _____ you from your God; and your sins have hidden His face from you, so that He will not hear."*

✓ **NOTE: The rich young ruler was told in the law of God, "You shall have no other gods before Me" (Exodus 20:3). He loved his money and possessions more than he loved God. Money was his god. Money in and of itself isn't evil; it's how most of us survive. So when does it become evil?**

10. What does the Bible tell us about money? 1 Timothy 6:10

*"For the _____  _____  _____ is a root of all kinds of evil, for which some have strayed from the faith in their greediness, and pierced themselves through with many sorrows."*

✓ **NOTE: Money is not the issue. The love of money is the problem. The rich young ruler loved his wealth more than he loved God, and that love of wealth produced a separation from God.**

11. So who does the Bible say has sinned? Romans 3:23

"For _____ have sinned and fall short of the glory of God."

✓ NOTE: Two problems occur here. First, sin separates us from God. Second, all have sinned and fallen short of the glory of God. So how do we fix the problem?

12. What two things does God tell us in the book of Acts to do? Acts 3:19

"_____ therefore and be _____ , that your sins may be blotted out, so that times of refreshing may come from the presence of the Lord."

✓ NOTE: The word "repent" means to change the mind. The word "convert" means to turn about. We have all sinned, which hurts our relationship with Christ by causing a separation between us. However, we are told to do something about it. Hopefully, when we realize we have done something wrong, we regret it. We must then confess our sins to Christ and ask Him for forgiveness.

13. If we do confess, what does Jesus tell us He will do? 1 John 1:9

"If we confess our sins, He is faithful and just to _____
_____ _____ _____
and to _____ _____ from all
_____ ."

✔ **NOTE: How great is that? Christ knows that we have a broken relationship with Him. He knows we broke it, but He willingly died on the cross to fix it. His act allows us to confess our sins to Him and be forgiven, so the separation doesn't have to be permanent. Sometimes in a relationship that was once good and somehow went bad, both parties have things in the way that just won't allow them to return to the relationship they once had. They just can't put their pride aside.**

**Christ isn't like that. He did nothing to break the relationship and is doing everything to fix it. He simply says in His Word, "Behold, I stand at the door and knock. If anyone hears my voice and opens the door, I will come in to him and dine with him, and he with Me" (Revelation 3:20). Is there something missing? Can it be to fix it all you have to do is open the door?**

Let's look at some principles in this lesson that are very important to rebuild the relationship that Christ desires to have with each of us.

**Points not to miss:**

1.  Before we study God's Word, we have learned that we need to ask for God's guidance (prayer).

2.  We also need to realize that sin separates us from God, and we are all sinners. (We're all separated from our Creator.)

3.  Don't start your relationship with a separation.

4.  Confess your sins, and ask God to forgive you.

5. Believe His Word that He will forgive and cleanse you from all unrighteousness.

6. Finally, God wants this relationship fixed even more than we do. **He died to fix it!** The question is: Will we use these principles in our lives to keep it?

May God bless you as you continue in your relationship with Him.

# Notes

# LESSON 4:

# Where Did That Come From?

A little girl watched her mother carefully prepare a pot roast so that when it was fully cooked, it would be just right. Just before she put it into the roasting pan, she cut off a little from each end. While it was in the oven cooking, the little girl asked her mother, "Why did you cut a little off each end before cooking?"

The girl's mother lovingly replied, "Dear, you will learn to cook from me just as I did from my mother, and my mother did from her mother. Great grandma always made the most wonderful pot roast. Just before it went into the oven to cook, she would cut off a little bit from each end. Since it always turned out just right, and so does mine, I do it just like great grandma did it." The child was satisfied, but all of sudden her mother wasn't. She wondered why her mother cut off a little from each end.

The next Sunday at the child's grandmother's house there was a special Sunday dinner because there were five living generations —the little girl, her mom, her grandma, her great grandma, and her great, great grandma—five generations in one room! After dinner and some conversation, the little girl's mother turned to her mother and said, "My daughter asked me while I was making pot roast why I cut off both ends. I said because I learned from you. But why do you do it?"

Her mother replied, "I learned it from my mother."

When great grandmother was asked, she gave the same response: "It's how mother taught me."

So all four generations asked the aged great, great grandmother, "Why did you cut off both ends from the pot roast before cooking? We all do it, but we really don't know why."

She thought for a moment, recalling all those years, and then a smile formed on her face. Then she broke out in laughter and said, "Way back then we only had one pot-roast pan, and it was a small one. I had to cut off a little from each end so it would fit into the pan. Nothing more and my children, and my children's children have been doing ever since not ever questioning why."

1. Knowledge is highly regarded in the Bible. How much worth does the Bible put on knowledge? Proverbs 8:10

*"Receive my instruction, and not silver, and knowledge rather than choice* _____ *."*

✔ **NOTE: Knowledge is regarded in the Bible as more valuable than gold, even choice gold. Proverbs 24:5 tells us that knowledge is strength, and Isaiah 33:6 tells us knowledge ensures stability. We could go on and on, but the point is that knowledge is highly rated throughout the Scriptures by God.**

**In Lesson 1, we learned the importance studying the Holy Scriptures. They will make us wise for salvation, and in Lesson 2, we learned we should never study the Scriptures without first asking for understanding (prayer). Now as we read the Bible, we will be gaining knowledge, which is another important part of our relationship with Christ.**

2. What is one reason why God's people are destroyed? Hosea 4:6

*"My people are destroyed for* _____ *of* _____*."*

✓ **NOTE: So knowledge is a key to salvation according to God's Word. God intends for us to gain spiritual knowledge in several ways. One is studying His Word; another way is through other people called prophets, teachers, pastors, and evangelists. Second Peter 1:21 explains that the people who wrote the Bible were inspired by God. However, immediately following 2 Peter 1:21, we are told something else happened.**

3.  What does God's Word tell us will come in among his people? Also, what are those people called? 2 Peter 2:1

*"But there were also* _____ _____ *among the people, even as there will be* _____ _____ *among you, who will secretly bring in destructive heresies, even denying the Lord who bought them, and bring on themselves swift destruction."*

✓ **NOTE: So be careful. God's Word can be trusted. However, some teachers, pastors, evangelists, etc. cannot be trusted. This is why God gave us instructions in His Word on how to test to see if these people are speaking the truth.**

4.  How are God's people supposed to speak? Isaiah 8:20

*"To the law and to the testimony! If they do not speak* _____ *to* _____ _____ *, it is because there is no light in them."*

✓ **NOTE: If a pastor, minister, or anyone teaches or preaches something that isn't according to God's Word, it is false, and there is no light or truth in them.** Since God has called people from all walks of life and has called them to teach and preach His gospel, we shouldn't turn our backs on what they have to say just because they are different from us. God does, however, expect us to test all teachings with His Word. For example, two of God's preachers, Paul and Silas, preached in a town called Berea. The Bereans listened carefully to what Paul and Silas said and then checked those teachings with the Scriptures.

5. When the preaching was over, what did these people do? Acts 17:11

*"These [the Bereans] were more fair-minded than those in Thessalonica, in that they received the word with all readiness, and _____ the _____ daily to _____ _____ whether these things were so."*

✓ **NOTE: Those in Thessalonica didn't check Paul and Silas' teachings with the Scriptures. Since they didn't like what was said, they rejected both Paul and Silas and their message. Earlier in this lesson we learned that Hosea 4:6 says, "My people are destroyed for lack of knowledge."**

6. Why didn't the people have knowledge? Hosea 4:6

*"Because you have _____ knowledge, I also will reject you from being priest for Me; because you have forgotten the law of your God, I also will forget your children."*

✓ **NOTE: The problem wasn't so much that people didn't know; the problem was that they rejected what the Lord gave them. When we reject what we read in God's Word, or reject people that God sends, or reject any form of light that God sends us, we put ourselves in grave spiritual danger. When we reject these things, we discard the knowledge that God is working to give us. God's Word is truth, and only the truth can set us free from sin (John 8:32).**

All truth can and should be tested. When Christ was tempted, He didn't say, "According to my mother," "According to my pastor," or "According to my church." He said, "It is written…" (Matthew 4:7).

So we should test what we learn with the Scriptures. Christ is our example if we claim to be Christians. The devil was trying to twist Scripture to lead Christ into sin, and the devil is still doing that today with you and me.

This lesson on knowledge may be the most important principle in forming a growing relationship with Christ—you likely have more against you than you realize. Just like the story in the beginning of this lesson, four generations found themselves cutting off the ends of their pot roast for the wrong reason. Quite harmless, I know, but thousands of Christians are rejecting knowledge because what they believe is what has been handed down by family, friends, or their pastor—by tradition. Although these people may be sincere, caring friends, the question is: where did they get their information? The information we take in should come from God's Word, and any other information should be tested by God's Word.

Tradition is a strong emotional tie, but God's Word tells us instead of walking according to tradition, walk in the light of His Word. If we're not in the light of His Word, we're in darkness. In closing, here's what the Bible says about how God wants us to walk with Him.

*"This is the message which we have heard from Him and declare to you, that God is light and in Him is no darkness at all. If we say that we have fellowship with Him, and walk in darkness, we lie and do not practice the truth. But if we walk in the light as He is in the light, we have fellowship with one another, and the blood of Jesus Christ His Son cleanses us from all sin."* (1 John 1:5–7)

Do we want to have a fellowship (sharing together) with Christ? Do we want to be cleansed from all sin? Do we want to be in the light? If so, embrace the truth as it comes, except knowledge, and be thankful for it. Don't reject knowledge and be in danger of being rejected by God. Base your Christian beliefs on "it is written," and God will bless you as you study His Word.

# LESSON 5:

# Don't Just Sit There

M any passages in the Bible tell us what kind of people God wants us to be. There is one principle that comes up over and over. One of those places is in the book of James where God tells us that there are people full of biblical knowledge. James' words are great because, as we learned in the last lesson, God is pleased when we equip ourselves with the knowledge that is in His Word. Then something happens, or should I say doesn't happen, that displeases Him.

In the book of James, chapter 1 verse 21, God is saying to get rid of the bad, the filth, and wickedness in our lives and to receive God's Word in our hearts so that He can save us. We have already examined that, but then in James 1:22, we see another principle emerging: "But be doers of the word, and not hearers only, deceiving yourselves." Verses 23 and 24 tell us, "For if anyone is a hearer of the word and not a doer, He is like a man observing his natural face in a mirror; for he observes himself, goes away, and immediately forgets what kind of man he was."

Can you imagine going out for the evening or meeting someone whom you admire? When you look in the mirror to see if your face is clean, you see it's filthy. Nevertheless, you go on your way anyway, not cleaning your face. What was the point of even looking in the mirror; it was a total waste of time! James 1:25 tells us, "But he who looks into the perfect law of liberty and continues in it, and is not a forgetful hearer but a doer of the work, this one will be blessed in what he does."

In verse 26, God gives us another example, and James uses the principle of how God's Word should change the way we talk to people, especially when we get upset with them. Christians should watch what they say, particularly when talking about others: "If anyone among you thinks he is religious, and does not bridle his tongue but deceives his own heart, this one's religion is useless." Here, God tells us that it's a waste of time to study His Word if our lives aren't going to change; we actually become useless. "Useless" means to not be any good for anything. Let's look at a common-sense example in James 2:15, 16: "If a brother or a sister is naked and destitute of daily food, and one of you says to them, 'Depart in peace, be warmed and filled,' but you do not give them the things which are needed for the body, what does it profit?"

If we see a person in need of clothes and food, and as Christians we recognize their need, but all we say is "Good luck, I hope you don't get cold and hungry," how does that help them? In effect, God is saying, "What good are you? What good is your religion? Why are you even calling yourself a Christian? You're not Christ-like." God wants men and women of action, men and women who desire to study, to search for knowledge, and then to put that knowledge of God's Word to work. Without putting that knowledge to work, your religion is useless.

1.  Does God recognize all those who call on Him? Matthew 7:21

"_____  _____ *who says to Me, 'Lord, Lord,' shall enter the kingdom of heaven."*

2.  But who does He recognize? Matthew 7:21

*"But he who _____ the will of My Father in heaven."*

✓ **NOTE: So it's not enough to acknowledge Christ and His Word, but we must be doers of the Word.**

3. What will God say to those people who say, "Lord, Lord"? Matthew 7:23

"And I will declare to them, _____ _____
_____ _____ ; *depart from Me, you who practice lawlessness!*"

✓ **NOTE: Plainly, God wants us to be good students of His Word. Studying is one of God's ways of communicating and allowing us to gain knowledge. But once we have been blessed by His Word, we are told to follow it—be doers, not hearers only. Christ gave us an example through His life of loving, caring for, and helping others. All He is saying to us is that if we want to be Christians, then follow My example.**

**Just so there is no confusion in this lesson, or in what God is saying in His Word about being doers not just hearers of His Word, God's Word is plain that we cannot work our way into heaven. No amount of doing will EARN any of us a place in His kingdom.**

4. There is something we can earn by our works. What is it? Romans 6:23

"For the _____ *of sin is death, but the gift of God is eternal life in Christ Jesus our Lord.*"

✓ **NOTE: So there is something we can earn—it's death. But eternal life with Christ cannot be earned; it's called a gift. Wages are earned, but a gift is free. So as we begin our walk with Christ through the power of His Word and guidance of the Holy Spirit, we will become changed just as the Bible says we will. Also, we'll begin to reflect Christ's character, showing kindness to others by allowing the Holy Spirit to change our ways as we receive the knowledge of Christ. As that happens, we must not let others tell us that we are trying to work our way to heaven. Paul, in the book of Romans, tells us that this is impossible. It is just as impossible for Christ to come into our lives and not be changed people.**

**I heard an aged pastor explain it this way, "Does a dog bark to become a dog? Or does a dog bark because it is a dog?" Personally, I wouldn't want a man or woman doing heart surgery on me to become a heart surgeon. I would want a man or woman to do heart surgery on me *because* he or she is a heart surgeon. Changing our lives and attitude to reflect Christ love is a byproduct of being a Christian. We don't do good things and change our lives to become a Christian. We do them because we are Christians.**

**Points not to miss:**

1. We need to have a desire to have a closer walk with Christ.

2. We need to believe the Bible is God's inspired Word.

3. We need to decide to study God's Word for a light unto our daily path.

4. We need to want to be doers not just hearers of God's Word.

5. We need to realize we can't do it alone; we need Christ in our lives.

6. We need to realize that there is nothing Christ wants more than to be in our lives.

So what's the problem? Let's put those principles to work and experience what God has planned for our lives. May God bless us as we reflect Christ's character in living out His Word.

# NOTES

# LESSON 6:

# Who's Way?

I remember a conversation that my brother had while he was running our business; actually, it was about the third conversation on the exact same subject with the exact same person—our secretary—who was probably a very good secretary. She had a lot of experience before working with us. She was also a very good person in general; she was kind, considerate, and thoughtful—all the things anyone would want in an employee who represented his or her business.

However, there was this one process with the bookwork that my brother wanted done in one particular way, and she wanted to do it in another. She was sure she did it just fine because she was accustomed to doing it in the way she had always done it. In her opinion there was no problem doing it her way. She enjoyed her job; she just wanted to do it her way.

Remember, this is the third conversation on this subject over a period of time. My brother would tell her, "I don't care how you used to do it in the past. Now I want it done this way." He did his best to explain why he wanted the task done that certain way and that for his business his way would be better. Then, as I remember, he said, "What you're doing isn't right for me or my business."

She was offended with that remark because she did her job well in her opinion. She felt that my brother was questioning her integrity, and she blurted out, "Look, I work hard for you; I don't make many mistakes; I get the job done; I get to work on time; I treat your business just like it was my very own!"

My brother replied just as forcefully, "That's the problem. I don't want you to treat it like it was your very own business; I want you to treat it like it's "mine"—because it isn't yours, it's mine. Eventually, the two parted ways, not as enemies but as two people with different ideas. But the big difference was the secretary tried to make the owner fit into her system, rather than fit into the owner's system.

Because of sin, we are a lost people in a lost world, but God has a perfect plan of salvation. God's Word has told us that plainly. However, many Christians believe that they have a good life, and they sincerely want God in their lives and in their plans. But the only way to have eternal life with Christ is to fit into His plan, not fit God into ours. Today, there are more than 3,000 different religions, dozens of ways people are baptized, all types of different worship styles, and all kinds of gods.

1. What does the Bible say about all different religions, faiths, and baptisms, etc.? Ephesians 4:4–6

*"There is one body and one Spirit, just as you were called in one hope of your calling; _____ Lord, _____ faith, _____ baptism; one God and Father of all, who is above all, and through all, and in you all."*

✓ **NOTE: God says "one way"; we say "many ways." Why are there so many different beliefs and so many different doctrines?**

2. What did the people do in the Apostle Paul's day when they didn't like the true or sound doctrine? 2 Timothy 4:3, 4

*"For the time will come when they will not endure sound doctrine, but according to their own desires, because they have itching ears, they will _____ up for _____ _____; and they will _____ _____ _____ away from the _____ , and be turned aside to fables."*

✓ **NOTE: When the people in Paul's day didn't like what he preached, which was the true and sound doctrine from the Scriptures, they would quit listening to him and find a teacher to teach or tell them what they wanted to hear. That problem has been around since the beginning of time and is growing stronger than ever today.**

3.  Why was Cain so angry with his brother Abel that he killed him? Genesis 4:4, 5

*"Abel also brought of the firstborn of his flock and of their fat. And the LORD _____ Abel and his offering, but He did not _____ Cain and his offering. And Cain was very angry, and his countenance fell."*

✓ **NOTE: Read Genesis 4:2–8. Here we find that Abel was a shepherd while Cain was a farmer (verse 2). After a while, instead of sacrificing a lamb like God told them to do, Cain made his offering to the Lord of the fruit of the ground that he had tilled.**

**Cain wanted to worship his way, not God's way, and when his brother Abel's offering was accepted and his wasn't, Cain became so angry that he killed his brother. Cain worked hard for what he grew, just like Abel worked hard**

*one lamb in ever church*

as a shepherd. Cain probably reasoned, "I toil hard for my fruit, I care for it, I weed it, I give the very best first fruits to God for an offering. Why won't God accept my offering?" The answer was because the offering was Cain's, not God's.

We need to follow God's plan, even in the way we worship Him. When we don't like what God's plan is, or what God's Word says, we have a decision to make. We can follow God's plan, make excuses, or find some way of changing God's Word so it's more convenient. Just remember that this method didn't work for Cain, and it won't work for any of us.

4. We may be sincere in our thoughts. We may really think our way is fine, but what does the Bible say about our ways and our thoughts? Isaiah 55:8, 9

*"'For my thoughts are not your thoughts, nor are your ways my ways,' says the LORD. "For as the heavens are higher than the earth, so are my ways _____ than your ways, and my thoughts than your thoughts."*

✓ NOTE: Too many times we try to compromise. Sometimes we think that if we do mostly what God has shown us, we do fairly well. But God isn't satisfied with part of us—He wants all of us. He gave all on the cross to save us, and He expects no less from us.

5. What was it that Noah did when the Lord instructed him? Genesis 6:22

*"Thus Noah did; according to* __ALL__ *that God commanded him, so he did."*

6. What did Peter and the disciples leave to follow Christ? Matthew 19:27

*"Then Peter answered and said to Him, "See, we have left* _everything_ *and followed You. Therefore what shall we have?"*

✓ **NOTE: In book after book of the Old and New Testaments, the men and women of God left all. But Christ didn't leave those who gave all with nothing. In Matthew 19:29, Jesus said those who gave up everything would receive 100 times more and eternal life. Christ doesn't require or want His people to be poor, or go without. He just requires all of us, not part of us.**

7. What did the Apostle John say he wanted for us? 3 John 1:2

*"Beloved, I pray that you may _____ in all things and be in health, just as your soul prospers."*

✓ **NOTE: God wants us to be complete Christians mentally, physically, and spiritually, and we will be if we give Him our all, just as He gave us His all. God's way is for the better, not worst. God only wants what's best for us even if we can't see it at the time, which is why we need to fit into His plan and not God into ours. Our request should be: "What will You have me to do?"**

**Points not to miss:**

1. God's ways are higher or better than any plan we could arrange.

2. We are not always going to understand why at first, but if we just trust and obey Him, we will be led to His understanding.

3. God's way will not always be popular with friends or family.

4. God's plans have never been in the majority, so don't look at what everyone else is doing and let that influence your decision. Noah was the minority. Moses was the minority. Christ Himself was crucified by the majority, and the crucifixion charge was lead by the church leaders! The majority was responsible for the death of Jesus, so be concerned with what's right not what most people are doing.

5. Being sincere by itself is not enough because we could be sincerely wrong and that could cost us everything. The only way to be safe in our decisions is to have them based on Scripture.

6. Remember: *"There is a way that seems right to a man, but its end is the way of death" (Proverbs 14:12).*

7. It's easy to look at the size of a church or the size of its membership. It's easy to say, "Lord, I do fairly well. How could holding onto just this one little thing be so bad?" The point is that God has a better plan for us, but before we can grab onto His plan, we have to let go of ours. All God is saying is, "I love you and want to spend eternal life with you. Will you trust Me to lead you in all things?" You're the only one who can answer that.

God wants what is best for us, and all we have to do is trust Him. Put away what we think or want, and hopefully our decision will be "Not as I will, but as You will" (Matthew 26:39). Those words were spoken by Christ Himself, and if we decide to be Christians, or Christ-like, we will do the same.

8. We should realize that God's way does matter. Jesus loves us very much, and He tells us in His Word, "If you love Me, keep My commandments" (John 14:15). When we say that it doesn't matter, and we don't have to keep God's commandments His way, we are in fact saying that we don't love Him.

May God bless you as you accept His way and His plan for your life.

# LESSON 7:

# Count the Cost

I hope by now that you're excited about studying the Bible—all for the right reasons. Hopefully, you want to build a relationship with Christ that will last through eternity. What a terrific goal to have. Prayer is essential to this process. Paul tells us in 1 Thessalonians 5:17 to "pray without ceasing." This means to always keep Christ within our frame of mind. Just like when a man who is in love with his wife (or vice versa) might say, "I think of her constantly; she is always on my mind."

By now you should understand that unfortunately sin came upon this planet, and it affects everyone. Nevertheless, we can rejoice because we serve a risen Savior who has made a way of escape. He died and made the ultimate sacrifice so we, through His blood, can be cleansed if we accept His gift of eternal life. We have learned that our relationship isn't based on size of church, tradition, or anything except what is written in His Holy Word.

As we prayerfully compare "line upon line," chapter with chapter, Old Testament with New Testament, we will be filled with His Spirit and be led to the path He has planned for us. We have also learned that once we see the path and direction He has laid out, we will walk that path. In other words we will be doers, not just readers or hearers. We have learned that we should desire to fit into God's plan, not expect Him to fit into ours. We are the ones who need changing, not Him.

We have learned many wonderful things, but we have not even scratched the surface. Christ wants us to spend eternity with Him in heaven where there will never be any more pain, sorrow, heartache, worry, or stress. We will walk hand in hand with our Savior, talk face to face just like Adam and Eve did before sin. When Christ was on this earth, He called his disciples to represent Him. We are also called to reflect His character to others. What a great opportunity! Let's open our Bibles to Matthew 10. In verse 1, Jesus had already chosen His twelve disciples.

1.  What did Jesus give to the twelve disciples? Matthew 10:1

*"And when He had called His twelve disciples to Him, He gave them _____ over unclean spirits, to cast them out, and to heal all kinds of sickness and all kinds of disease."*

✓ **NOTE: Notice that the Scripture goes on to say that they had power to heal the sick. Can you imagine what a blessing that would be? After naming the Twelve, Jesus gave them His final instructions: "Heal the sick, cleanse the lepers, raise the dead, cast out demons. Freely you have received, freely give" (Matthew 10:8).**

**Through His example, Jesus showed the disciples what to do to help others. Thus far, life had been exciting for the disciples. They left everything to be with Jesus, and He taught them to love one another. He showed mercy to all by restoring sight to the blind (Matthew 9:27, 28). He also restored speech to the mute and cast out demons (Matthew 9:32, 33). In Matthew 9:35 we read, "Then Jesus went about all cities and villages, teaching in their synagogues [churches], preaching the gospel of the kingdom,**

and healing every sickness and every disease among the people."

Can you picture in your mind what a wonderful sight that would have been? The disciples had an opportunity to follow in the footsteps of Jesus; what an opportunity that would be! Just imagine how excited and eager they must have been to start sharing what Christ had shared with them. Jesus also explained a very caring and important principle to which we should pay attention.

2. To what did Jesus compare the disciples? What are they expected to meet? Matthew 10:16

*"Behold, I send you out as _____ in the midst of _____. Therefore be wise as serpents and harmless as doves."*

✓ NOTE: Jesus went on to say in verse 17 we may be scourged or punished for preaching the gospel, so none of us will be loved by everybody. In fact, many will hate us for following Christ, and they will try to do us harm (Matthew 10:22, 23).

3. From where does some of the harm or the enemies come? Matthew 10:36

*"And 'a man's enemies will be those of his _____ _____.'"*

4. How strong is our love for Christ to be? Matthew 10:37

*"He who loves _____ or _____ more than Me is not worthy of Me. And he who loves _____ or _____ more than Me is not worthy of me."*

✓ **NOTE: How strong? Simply, Jesus puts us first in all that He did and does for us. He gave His all, including His life. We need to put Him first in our lives.**

5. How well does God know us? Matthew 10:30

*"But the very _____ of your _____ are all numbered."*

✓ **NOTE: Jesus knows all about us—every detail, every thought, every strength, and every weakness. He shared with us that He cares for the sparrow and that our worth is valued at so much more. So we don't need to worry because He will always be there for us (Matthew 10:31, 32). Being a Christian means to be Christ-like in the way we treat others and in all that we do. There isn't anything about us that won't be affected once we have Christ in our lives.**

6. What part of our lives will be affected once we use our lives to glorify God? 1 Corinthians 10:31

*"Therefore, whether you _____ or _____, or _____ you do, do all to the glory of God."*

✓ NOTE: This counsel will effect change in our lives. God will lead this change if we let Him, and it will be a wonderful change. The change will affect everything: eating, drinking, things we watch, things we say, hobbies; absolutely everything in our lives will change for the better. Christ promised that in His Word.

However, Christ loves enough to be honest with us and has told us that there is a cost involved in following Him. For example, we may run into opposition with friends or family because they may not understand how having Christ is life-changing. The fact is that some people are not going to be happy and won't like the new you.

The devil definitely won't be happy and will try to persuade us to look away from our relationship with Christ, so things won't be all easy. Christ spent a lot of time in His Word warning us so that we know what to expect and won't be surprised when we see some of these things happen.

God does not force us to love Him. We have a choice. God desires that we love Him because He first loved us and is worthy of our love. He wants us to obey Him because we have an intelligent appreciation of His wisdom, justice, love, and generosity. All who understand God in this way will be drawn toward Him in admiration and will **desire** to follow Him.

Someone suggested a warning label to go along with the Bible. It went something like this:

---

**—Caution—**

This book will go against some of your current ideas and beliefs. It will be easier to reject new ideas than to let go of what you are comfortable with. It may affect those who you hang out with (family, friends, etc.). It may affect your relationship with your church if you have one. If you are afraid of being changed by reading this book, then now would be a good time to put it down.

---

Christ simply put it like this: "So likewise, whoever of you does not forsake all that he has cannot be My disciple" (Luke 14:33). Those that accept Him as their Lord and Savior are promised blessings and joy beyond comprehension. There is no doubt it will be worth it all. But once again, the choice is yours—yours and mine individually.

May God bless you as you continue to study His Word.

# NOTES

## Answers to Lesson 1: Why Study?

1. Holy, Spirit

2. Salvation

3. Eternal, life

4. Approved, to, God

5. Doctrine, reproof, correction, instruction, righteousness

6. Lamp, light

7. Works

8. More, abundantly

9. Come, to, Me, kingdom, of, heaven

*Studying With Purpose* Promise:

*Let not your heart be troubled; you believe in God, believe also in Me. In My Father's house there are many mansions; if it were not so, I would have told you. I go to prepare a place for you. And if I go and prepare a place for you, I will come again and receive you to Myself; that where I am, there you maybe also.* (John 14:1–3)

God is preparing us a place to live with Him for eternity. Let's make it our purpose to live with Him.

## Answers to Lesson 2: How Do I Begin?

1. His, Spirit

2. Prayer, requests

3. Blind, blind

4. Precept, precept, precept, precept, upon, line, upon

5. Examples, admonition

6. Newborn, babes

*Studying With a Purpose* Promise:

*Come to Me, all you who labor and are heavy laden, and I will give you rest. Take my yoke upon you and learn from Me, for I am gentle and lowly in heart, and you will find rest for you souls. For My yoke is easy and My burden is light.* (Matthew 11:28–30)

Christ simply said, "Come unto Me." He gave us the invitation; it's up to us to respond.

## Answers to Lesson 3: What Happened?

1. Running, knelt, what, shall, I, do, eternal, life
2. Keep, the, commandments
3. All, these, kept, still, lack
4. Sell, what, you, have
5. He, went, away, sorrowful
6. Very, good
7. Hid, themselves
8. Sin, is, lawlessness
9. Separated
10. Love, of, money
11. All
12. Repent, converted
13. Forgive, us, our, sins, cleanse, us, unrighteousness

*Studying With a Purpose* Promises:

*The LORD has appeared of old to me, saying: "Yes, I have loved you with an everlasting love; therefore with lovingkindness I have drawn you. (Jeremiah 31:3)*

*For God so loved the world that He gave His only begotten Son, that whoever believes in Him should not perish but have everlasting life. (John 3:16)*

God has loved us with an everlasting love and gave up everything, even His own life, for you and me. In drawing us to Him, we need to allow our love to be drawn so we can forever be with Him.

## Answers to Lesson 4: Where Did That Come From?

1. Gold

2. Lack, knowledge

3. False, prophets, false, teachers

4. According, this, word

5. Searched, Scriptures, find, out

6. Rejected

*Studying with a Purpose* Promise:

*Let it be known to you all, and to all the people of Israel, that by the name of Jesus Christ of Nazareth, whom you crucified, whom God raised from the dead, by Him this man stands here before you whole. This is the stone. This is the "stone which was rejected by you builders, which has become the chief cornerstone." Nor is there salvation in any other, for there is no name under heaven given among men by which we must be saved.* (Acts 4:10–12)

The children of Israel rejected Christ because of their traditions and selfish ambitions. God's Word tells us there is no other name than Christ by which we can be saved. The Bible, and the Bible only, should be our guide.

## Answers To Lesson 5: Don't Just Sit There

1. Not, everyone

2. Does

3. I, never, knew, you

4. Wages

*Studying with a Purpose* Promise:

*Now the man from whom the demons had departed begged Him that he might be with Him. But Jesus sent him away saying, "Return to your own house, and tell what great things God has done for you." And he went his way and proclaimed throughout the whole city what great things Jesus had done for him.* (Luke 8:38, 39)

In another part of the Bible (Matthew 9:5, 6), Jesus healed a man who had been crippled for years. Jesus said, "Take up your bed" and walk. When Christ comes into our lives, He expects us to impart His love to other lives, "Tell what great things God has done for you." Don't just sit there; get up and walk. May God bless you as you begin your Christ-filled walk.

## Answers To Lesson 6: Who's Way?

1. One, one, one

2. Heap, themselves, teachers, turn, their, ears, truth

3. Respected, respect

4. Higher

5. All

6. All

7. Prosper

*Studying with a Purpose* Promises:

*And Jesus, walking by the Sea of Galilee, saw two brothers, Simon called Peter, and Andrew his brother, casting a net into the sea; for they were fishermen. Then He said to them, "Follow Me and I will make you fishers of men." They immediately left their nets and followed Him.* (Matthew 4:18–20)

*Jesus said to him, "I am the way, the truth, and the life. No one comes to the Father except through Me.* (John 14:6)

There is only one way—that way is Christ. We need to rearrange our lives and think toward His will, not the other way around.

## Answers To Lesson 7: Count The Cost

1. Power

2. Sheep, wolves

3. Own, household

4. Father, mother, son, daughter

5. Hairs, head

6. Eat, drink, whatever

*Studying with a Purpose* Promise:

*Enter by the narrow gate; for wide is the gate and broad is the way that leads to destruction, and there are many who go in by it. Because narrow is the gate and difficult is the way which leads to life, and there are few who find it.* (Matthew 7:13, 14)

With only two ways, the only real question is, "Which will you choose?" Christ Himself chose to save a lost and dying world, but it wasn't easy for Him. The cross wasn't easy; it was difficult. But to Christ it was worth it to be with us, you and me. Are we willing to walk the difficult path for Christ—the same path He walked for us? To me it's worth it, but I can't decide for you. But you can!

I pray you receive a Christ-filled blessing as you study God's Word and form an everlasting relationship with Him.

# Continuing Your Studies

S tudying the Bible is very important to our relationship with Christ. Using Bible-based principles on how to study is just as important. I hope you have come to realize this truth as you have studied the seven principles mapped out in this book.

The reason why there are so many different opinions on life-changing topics is because many people don't let the Bible interpret the Bible. When a Bible principle goes against what is comfortable, many times a person, or even a whole church, will bend that principle to fit his or her current lifestyle. After a while, others just assume that's what it must mean, and they don't read or study to test those Bible principles they have been taught.

The seven principles you have studied are just the beginning, and they need to be used every time we study God's Word. Bible truths have been distorted since sin began. Just one example is when Eve was tempted in the Garden of Eden, way back in the book of Genesis. God said that if we would disobey, we would die (Genesis 2:17). The devil tempted Eve saying, "You will not surely die" (Genesis 3:4). Ever since that devilish lie, some people have been fooled into thinking that dying isn't really dying; it's just the beginning of eternal life. What's even worse, some of the same people believe that it doesn't matter how they live on this earth (living for Christ or living for self). When we die (which to them isn't really dead), we immediately spend eternity with God. It would be a good and comforting story if it was Bible-based, but it's not.

Your eternal life may depend on your Bible knowledge, so at least get it from the Bible. A good place to start furthering your relationship with Christ through study is right here. Following is a compiled list of topics for study, starting with the first and ending with the last, or by choosing your own order. These topics were chosen after observing many different denominations and religions, and many if not all believe in these topics. The problem is that they have different ideas and conclusions on such topics—most of which are based on tradition—these studies are based solely on the Bible.

For example, most Christians believe in Christ, but some don't believe He is really the Son of God. Another topic is heaven; almost all religions believe in heaven, but the truth about where it is and how to get there varies greatly. So if you're planning to go to heaven, it is important how and what you believe. Another topic is forgiveness. Most Christians believe it's important, but some believe we go to God in prayer and ask Him for forgiveness, and others believe we can bypass God and ask man to forgive us. If eternal life depends on who forgives (and it does), isn't that a topic worth studying?

So look over the list, and let's get started. Some topics may be surprising, or even startling. Take comfort in the fact that we don't have to believe in the pages of this book, or this study, or as author, my ideas and the opinions. Instead, I suggest that you study your Bible, and let the Bible—the Bible only—be used to prove each and every topic. Remember: "To the law and to the testimony! If they speak not according to this word, it is because there is no light in them" (Isaiah 8:20). Don't let your Bible belief be one of darkness; use God's Word to back up what you believe, and walk in His light.

May God bless you as you choose from the ten topics to continue your relationship with Christ.

1. Always Trusted, Never Busted
   (Can You Really Trust the Bible?)

2. Too Bad, Too Good, Too Late
   (Salvation Won't Work for Me.)

3. Don't Just Stand There, Do Something
   (Necessary Steps for Forgiveness)

4. You Have Never Seen Anything Like It
   (Heaven)

5. Forgiven, Now Forget It?
   (Once Saved, Always Saved)

6. You Died for Me; I'll Live for You
   (Sanctification, Living the Life)

7. Come Unto Me, and I Will Give You Rest
   (Sabbath)

8. Mine, All Mine ... Isn't It?
   (Tithe and Offerings)

9. Two by Two, or Two by Seven?
   (Diet and Health)

10. WWW Baptism
    (The Why Where When of Baptism)

To order these studies, please contact Remnant Publications on-line at www.remnantpublications.com or by phone at 800-423-1319.

# Personal Journal

Now that you have begun to study with a purpose, this part of the book will help you focus on that goal. Your prayer life might be improved as well if you have a place to write down your prayer praises and requests. Many of the people you meet and those you already know could use prayer. They might even ask you to keep them in your prayers because of a sickness, a personal problem, or a struggle they're going through. If you are anything like me, it is easy to forget something now and then, but if you have a list right at your fingertips, it could be a useful tool to get more out of your prayer life.

Also, this is a good place to keep track of answered prayers. Many times in my life when I'm feeling a little depressed, and my faith isn't what it should be, looking back and reminding myself of past victories by turning to Christ is encouraging.

Another use for this journal is a place to write down spiritual goals and progress toward those goals. One goal might be to lead someone to Christ by being a spiritual friend or sharing how the Lord has blessed in your own life. If the Lord has blessed you through this book, then you could share that.

This is also a good place to jot down a verse or passage of Scripture that has special meaning to you. As you study, there will be texts that will jump out at you and serve in all aspects of your life. So writing them in your journal not only keeps them close, but writing them also helps in remembering them.

You may have many more reasons of your own to use this journal. Through its use, I hope you will both enjoy it and use it to further your journey with Christ.

May God bless you as your walk continues.

# Personal Journal

# PERSONAL JOURNAL

# PERSONAL JOURNAL

# PERSONAL JOURNAL

# PERSONAL JOURNAL

PERSONAL JOURNAL